T0116994

STUART LEE

MAGIC ACES

A COMPLETE ROUTINE
OF
AMAZING CARD TRICKS

ALL YOU NEED
TO KNOW

ISBN: 978-1-4269-6201-1 (sc)
ISBN: 978-1-4269-6202-8 (e)

Trafford rev. 05/18/2011

 www.trafford.com

North America & international
toll-free: 1 888 232 4444 (USA & Canada)
phone: 250 383 6864 ✦ fax: 812 355 4082

CONTENTS

INTRODUCTION

IN CARD MAGIC THE TRICKS involving the use of the Aces have always been foremost among those that impress spectators.

Try an experiment on yourself or a spectator. Deal out face-up onto a table four cards, including one Ace. Immediately, turn all the cards face-down. Which card stood out from the others? It was, of course, the Ace.

A King, a Queen, and a Jack are certainly more colourful than the Aces, and they and all the other cards of the pack have more detail on them than an Ace, but it is the Aces that create the strongest impression. They are easily recognised and remembered by a spectator, who is always intrigued when one or more of them is produced from the pack in a surprising way. There are many reasons for this: as the Aces have the least detail on them than any of the cards in the pack they have the strongest visual impact; in almost all card games they are the winning card or they are the cards that are used to form the winning hand; they are the only cards that in some card games can have a high or a low value depending on the requirement of the hand; in many fields of endeavour "an Ace" is the best there is; and in tennis "an Ace" is an un-playable first serve. Given all these attributes and associations it is little wonder that the Aces command the immediate attention of the spectator.

This book sets out complete instructions for the performance of a routine of card tricks – all of them involving effects based on the revelation of the Aces in a variety of surprising ways.

Very little skill in card manipulation is required to perform the routine and any manipulations that are required are fully explained and described in the chapter "*Handling and Sleights-of-Hand*". With regard to the sleights-of-hand the routine can be performed without the use of any as the tricks are self-working – the sleights-of-hand being used, in almost all cases, only to create the illusion that the cards are being indiscriminately mixed.

The whole routine lasts for approximately 25-30 minutes.

For the reader whose appetite for card magic as described in this book is whetted their attention is drawn to a companion book "*Old Wine In A New Bottle*" (Trafford, Bloomington, 2010) by the same author. This gives complete instructions for a routine of "classic" card tricks re-worked to produce spectacular effects.

As in that book, it is necessary to begin with some definitions of the terms used in describing the cards and in describing the manipulations of the cards. These are re-produced below:

All 52 cards together are *the pack* or *the deck*

Any part of the pack is *a packet*

A hand (of cards) is a packet that has been dealt to or given to a spectator

To deal consecutively is to deliver to each hand in turn one card until the deal is completed. *To deal the hands individually* is to deliver all the cards required to one hand before proceeding to deal the next hand.

To count cards reversing their order is to place each card as it is counted on top of the previous card. *To count cards without reversing their order* is to place each card as it is counted beneath the previous card.

Face-down and *face-up* cards are self-evident terms, the face of a card being its value and suit.

The long edge of a card, packet, or pack is *the side*.

The short edge of a card, packet, or pack is *the end*.

Front and *forward* and *outward* are away from you, and *rear* and *backward* and *inward* are towards you.

Left and *right* are from your viewpoint.

With the end of the cards or pack pointing towards the spectators, *the outer end* is the end pointing towards the spectators, and *the inner end* is the end pointing towards you.

With the cards or pack held in the right hand and with the outer end pointing towards the spectators, the outer side is to the right and the inner side is towards the left. Similarly, if the outer side is pointing towards the spectators the outer end is to the right and the inner end is to the left.

With the cards or pack held in the left hand and the outer end pointing towards the spectators the outer side is to the left and the inner side is to the right. Similarly, if the outer side is pointing towards the spectators the outer end is to the left and the inner end is to the right.

The fingers are: *first* (or *index*), *second*, *third* (or *ring*), and *fourth* (or *little*, sometimes referred to as "*the pinky*").

To cut and complete is to take a packet of cards from the top of the pack and to place what was the bottom of the pack on top of it. With the cards in hand the same outcome is achieved by *the undercut*, where the bottom part of the pack is cut away and transferred to the top of the pack.

To cull is to extract a card or cards (either openly or secretly) from the rest of the cards in a pack or packet.

An *out-jogged* or *up-jogged* card or packet is a card or packet positioned in the pack so that the card or packet projects from the pack.

A break is a small gap or opening formed secretly within a packet or pack at either the inner end or at the inner corner of the inner side. The former is held by the tip of the thumb of the hand holding the cards and the latter by the tip of the little finger of the hand holding the cards (and for this reason it is sometimes referred to as "*a pinky break*").

A bridged card is a card that has been subjected to pressure either at the sides or the ends to produce a curve along its length or across its width. A forward curve to the face of a card is a *convex bridge*, and a rearward curve to the face of a card is a *concave bridge*.

Having studied these basic definitions you should be able to follow the instructions for the performance of the tricks, the handling of the cards, and the sleights-of-hand with ease. It is appropriate now to turn our attention to the cards themselves.

There are innumerable manufacturers of playing cards and therefore a vast variety of packs available. They come in many shapes, styles and sizes. Although the majority are rectangular in shape it is possible to find packs of circular cards and even some with triangular- or diamond-shaped cards. They may have backs that are plain or patterned, single- or multi-coloured, and at least one pack produced is transparent, the face of the cards being visible through the back of the card. There are giant-sized cards and miniature cards. All of them can be, and have been, used in card magic but the cards most favoured by performers fall into two main styles and sizes. They are usually referred to as Poker-size packs and Bridge-size packs. Each of these has distinct features and advantages and these are discussed in the companion book already referred to above: "*Old Wine In A New Bottle*". For ease of reference, the relevant section of that book is re-produced below.

The larger of the two sizes is the *Poker-size* and an example of the Poker-size is the "*Bicycle Rider Back*" pack produced by the U.S. Playing Card Co. It is obtainable in magic shops and some stationery shops and comes in a variety of coloured backs. Examples of the Bridge-size pack are the "*No 1*" pack by the Waddington Playing Card Co. Ltd. (Winning Moves UK Ltd.) and the "*Standard*" playing cards produced and sold by W.H. Smith. These are widely available in the United Kingdom and come either Red-backed or Blue-backed.

The "*Bicycle Rider Back*" pack has two indexes on the face of each card, ie. the value and suit of the card are shown at the top left and at the bottom right corners. The Waddington "*No 1*" pack and the W.H. Smith pack are four indexed cards with the value and suit of the cards shown at all four corners of the face of each card. (Waddington also produces a four indexed "*No 1 Poker Deck*".) An advantage of a four indexed pack is that irrespective of whether the face of the pack is fanned or spread from left to right or right to left the indexes of the cards are equally observable. Additionally, some performers find the smaller Bridge-size cards easier to handle. However, most performers prefer to use the "*Bicycle Rider Back*" packs as among the many advantages they give are the variety of colours for the backs, the fact that they can be obtained with blank faces, blank backs, doubled-faced, double-backed, and as a miniature size with red, blue or green backs in a design identical to the full-sized packs. They are also available in a number of specially prepared packs to perform particular tricks and effects.

A fourth range of playing cards merits attention and that is the "*Classic*" design produced by the Austrian company Piatnik. They are Bridge-sized cards available in back designs in red or blue and also in special packs (ie. blank backs, blank faces, etc.).

For completeness it should also be noted that W.H. Smith produce and sell miniature "*Patience*" packs in identical back design and colour to their "*Standard*" packs and also a Poker-size pack – this latter pack being a card with two extra-large indexes on the face of the cards.

The introductory chapter of my book "*Old Wine In A New Bottle*" concludes with some words of advice for the beginner in card magic and they are worth being repeated here:

Study the descriptions of the handling and presentation carefully before you attempt to perform them.

Go through the manipulations and presentation slowly on the first attempts.

Try not to look at your hands when shuffling or performing a manipulation.

Perform the manipulations and presentations over and over again in practice and only perform a trick for others when you are totally confident of your ability to do so successfully.

If necessary, distract the attention of the spectators away from the cards by diverting their attention elsewhere. This can be done by talking to them directly and requiring a response or by giving them something to do or to look at.

Do not be afraid when the occasion requires it to perform some manipulations openly. It is surprising what can go unnoticed provided it is done boldly and the attention of the spectators distracted by directing it elsewhere.

When you are performing a trick do not rush the presentation. You know the trick and the effect you are attempting, but, hopefully, it is the first time the spectators have seen the trick performed and to rush the presentation would be to confuse them.

As a general rule, never repeat a trick in the same performance. Exceptions are where the same effect or outcome can be achieved by different means or when the mechanics of the trick are such that it is impossible for the spectators to determine how the effect is brought about.

And **never ever** reveal how an effect has been achieved.

PREPARATION

TO PERFORM THE ROUTINE you require two packs of cards of identical design but with different coloured backs, eg, one blue, one red.

With regard to your choice of packs you should note that the "*Bicycle Rider Back*" packs and the W.H. Smith cards are readily available in a "miniature" or approximately half-sized pack with back designs and colour identical to the full-sized packs. These packs can be used to strengthen the presentation of one of the tricks in the routine ("*Telepathic Aces*") although the trick can be performed using only the full-sized packs.

You should also note that whatever packs you decide to use for the routine you will need four Joker cards for each pack to perform the trick "*You Must Be Joking*" and you will therefore need to purchase two packs of each back colour.

Having decided on your choice of packs the two packs required for the routine should be ordered (or "*stacked*") in preparation for the first tricks of the routine ("*Finding The Aces*" and "*You Must Be Joking*"). Obviously, if such preparation is not possible then these two tricks cannot be performed. They should be replaced by tricks from the chapter *"Adaptations and Alternatives"*.

To prepare the packs you should begin by extracting the Joker cards and any extraneous cards from the packs. Discard the extraneous cards (eg. scoring-cards, promotional cards, etc) and place the Blue-backed Jokers with the Blue-backed pack and the Red-backed Jokers with the Red-backed pack.

You now arrange (or stack) the packs for the routine as follows:

    a.   First take the Blue-backed pack and order the face-down pack as follows:
        (Top): Red Ace – the 4 Jokers – any 11 cards – Black Ace – any 18 cards – Black Ace – any 9 cards – Red Ace – any 9 cards and the bridged card (or any 10 cards if you are not using a bridged card). *(For an explanation on how to prepare and use a bridged card see the relevant section in the chapter on "Handling and Sleights-of-Hand".)*

    b.   Place the pack in the appropriate carton.

    c.   Now take the Red-backed pack and order the face-down pack in exactly the same way.

An alternative method of ordering the pack, which is easier to recall from memory, is to extract the Aces from the pack and to proceed as follows: in the face-down pack place an Ace at the following positions: 12th card, 31st card, and 41st card. Then place the four Joker cards face-down on top of the pack and the final Ace face-down on top of the Jokers. If you are using a bridged card ensure that this card is the bottom card of the arranged pack.

With the packs so arranged you are now ready to perform the routine of tricks.

THE ROUTINE

PRESENTING THE CARDS

1. Begin with the two prepared packs of cards in their cartons on the table.

2. The spectator or spectators are asked to choose which pack they wish you to use. Take this pack out of its carton, taking care not to disturb the pre-arranged order of the cards.

3. If you are not using a bridged card proceed directly to paragraph 4 below. If you are using a bridged card you may now perform "a false mix of the pack" or you may, if you wish, merely allow the spectator to "cut and complete" the pack before you finally cut the bridged card to the bottom of the pack. *(For an explanation of how to perform "a false mix of the pack" and how to use the bridged card see the relevant sections in the chapter on "Handling and Sleights-of-Hand".)*

4. Turn the pack face-up and spread out the cards to show the mix, taking care not to display the bottom five cards of the face-up pack, which are the four Jokers and an Ace. Once the pack has been displayed turn it face-down and place it on the table.

5. Explain that as all the tricks you are going to perform involve the "magic Aces" you will need a little help to find them.

FIRST TRICK: *"Finding The Aces"*

1. Challenge a spectator to cut off exactly half of the pack from the top of the face-down pack and, when he or she has done so, to hand it to you. To confirm that it is half of the pack deal the cards out face-down into a pile on the table, counting them out aloud as you do so (*you are, in fact, also reversing their order*). If there are 26 cards congratulate the spectator on the accuracy of his or her cut. If there are more than 26 cards stop the deal at 26 and return the extra cards face-down to the top of the rest of the pack without disturbing their order. If you have less than 26 cards make the total up to 26 by taking cards in turn off the top of the rest of the pack and placing them face-down in turn on the top of the pile of counted cards.

2. Take the face-down pile of cards you have counted out and neaten them up. You then challenge the spectator again to cut the pile exactly in half. When he or she has done so count out the cards. If there are 13 cards, congratulate the spectator. If there are 10 or more merely comment on this. If there are less than 10 make up the number to any number the spectator chooses above 10 by taking the necessary number off the top of the pile. Then take the remaining cards and place them aside.

3. Now instruct the spectator to take the number of cards arrived at and to add the two digits together to give a single digit number (ie. 14 = 1 + 4 = 5). The spectator then takes the pile of cards from the table, counts down in the pile to the card at that number and then takes

the card at that position in the pile. (*It will be an Ace.*) Place the card face-up on the table.

4. Take all the other cards of the pile from which the spectator has been counting and place them all face-down on top of the cards you placed aside at paragraph 2 above. Then pick up this consolidated pile of cards and place them **beneath** the other half of the pack. (*Note: If these moves have been correctly performed the bottom cards of the face-down pack are now the four Joker cards and an Ace.*)

5. You now invite the spectator to think of and state any number he or she wishes between 10 and 20. When he or she has done so deal off face-down from the top of the face-down pack that number of cards into a face-down pile. Take the two digits of the number he or she gave and add them together to give a single digit number. The spectator then takes the pile of cards, counts down to that number, and takes the card at that position. (*It will be an Ace.*) Place it face-up by the side of the other Ace.

6. Take all the other cards and place them face-down **on top** of the rest of the face-down pack.

7. Next invite the spectator to think of and state any number her or she wishes between 20 and 30 and for that number repeat the procedure described at paragraph 5 above. (*The spectator will arrive at the third Ace.*) Place it face-up by the side of the other Aces and place all the other cards face-down on top of the rest of the face-down pack.

8. Remark that all you need now is the fourth and final Ace
   – and, as you are doing so, take the bottom card of the
   pack and place it face-down by the side of the three face-
   up Aces. Instruct the spectator to turn the card face-up.
   (*When he or she does so it will be the fourth Ace.*)

SECOND TRICK: *"You Must Be Joking"*

1. Observe that as you now have the Aces you can get on with the tricks.

2. Take the pack, place it face-down on the table, and instruct the spectator to place the Aces face-down on top of the pack. Then instruct the spectator to cut off about the top ¾ of the pack and to place it to the right of the other cards (*from his or her point of view*). He or she should then cut off about ¾ of the cards of this second pile and place these to the right of the other two piles (*again from his or her point of view*). Finally, he or she should create a fourth pile by cutting off about the top half of the third pile. This pile he or she places to the right of the other three piles.

3. You now have (*from your point of view*):
    Pile A   Pile B   Pile C   Pile D
    (*Note: Pile D is the original bottom ¼ or so of the pack and Pile A is the original top ¼ or so of the pack.*)

4. There are now two ways of proceeding with the trick – the first involves the use of sleights-of-hand, the second does not. If you wish to use the first finish proceed directly to paragraphs 5 and 6 below; if you choose not to use sleights-of-hand proceed directly to paragraphs 7-11 below.

5. Place Pile A on Pile C and place Pile B on Pile D. Then place Pile AC on Pile BD. Then instruct the spectator to cut off about the top half of the face-down pack

and to place it by the side of the bottom "half" of the pack. Take what was the top half of the pack in your left hand and the bottom half of the pack in your right hand and riffle shuffle them together. In performing the shuffle ensure that the bottom four cards of the right-hand packet fall first as a block and that the top four cards of the left-hand packet fall last as a block. (*For an explanation of this shuffle see the relevant sections in the chapter on "Handling and Sleights-of-Hand".*) Having performed the shuffle invite the spectator to cut the face-down pack again. You then repeat the shuffle described above. When the second shuffle has been completed hand the face-down pack to the spectator and instruct him or her to deal out four piles of face-down cards, dealing a card to each pile in turn.

6. Now ask the spectator what he or she would say if you forecast that the bottom card of each pile would be an Ace. Whatever the reply, say that you imagine it might be: "You must be joking!" Ask the spectator to turn over *the top card of each pile.* (*They will be Jokers.*) Then ask the spectator to deal face-up each pile in turn. (*The bottom card will be an Ace.*)

7. Instruct the spectator to turn Pile B face-up, and then to turn Pile C face-up. You then place Pile A on Pile C, then Pile B on Pile D, and then Pile AC on Pile BD. Having done this, instruct the spectator to cut off about the top half of the face-down pack and place it by the side of the bottom "half" of the pack. When he or she has done this, take the two packets and riffle shuffle them into each other. (*For an explanation of this shuffle see the relevant sections in the chapter on "Handling and Sleights-of-Hand".*)

8. Now hand the pack to the spectator and get him or her to deal out the pack into two piles – one of the face-up cards and the other of face-down cards. When this has been done hand the face-down cards to the spectator and put the face-up cards aside. Now instruct the spectator to deal four piles of face-down cards, dealing a card to each pile in turn.

9. When the deal is completed ask the spectator what he or she would have to say if you forecast that the bottom card of each pile would be an Ace. Irrespective of the response say that you imagine it would be "You must be joking!" *Instruct the spectator to turn over each pile.* (*The cards revealed will be Jokers.*) Then get the spectator to take each pile in turn and to deal out the cards from the top of the face-up pile. (*Each deal should finish with an Ace.*)

THIRD TRICK: *"Card Sharper's Aces"*

1. Instruct the spectator to sort out the Aces and the Jokers
    and to put the Jokers in their appropriate carton. As he
    or she is doing this you collect the rest of the cards.

2. Now take the Aces from the spectator and place them
    on the table in a face-up pile with the two Black Aces
    on the top of the pile. Then take each Ace in turn and
    place it face-down in the face-down pack, pushing each
    into the pack at the outer end, which you hold towards
    the spectators. In placing the cards into the pack the
    first two Aces (the Black Aces) should be placed in the
    bottom half of the pack and the last two Aces (the Red
    Aces) in the top half of the pack – the final Red Ace
    being placed in the pack as close to the top of the pack as
    possible, but not on the top. Now cut away the bottom
    ¼ of the face-down pack and place it on top of the pack.
    Then cut away the bottom half of the pack and place
    that packet on top of the pack. Finally, place the pack
    face-down on the table.

3. If you are not using a bridged card and sleights-of-hand
    in the performance of the routine proceed directly to
    paragraph 5 below.

4. If you are using a bridged card and sleights-of-hand
    there is an alternative method of handling to that set
    out at paragraph 2. If you wish to use it proceed as
    follows: take some time in explaining that you are going
    to demonstrate the way in which card-sharpers can
    manipulate cards to their advantage and that for this

you need only three Aces. As you are doing so collect the cards as described at paragraph 1 above and cut the bridged card to the bottom of the face-down pack and then place two face-down cards below it. Then instruct the spectator to place one of the Red Aces at the top, or bottom, or in the "middle" of the pack as described in the relevant section of the chapter on *Handling and Sleights-of-Hand*". The spectator may then cut and complete the pack, at will. Finally, you cut the bridged card to the bottom of the pack, thus placing the Red Ace as the third card from the top in the face-down pack. Proceed now directly to paragraph 6 below.

5. Take some time in explaining that you are now going to demonstrate the way in which card-sharpers can manipulate cards to their advantage. While you are doing so pick up the pack from the table, turn it face-up and go through it, taking out the Aces as you come to them. Explain that to perform the demonstration you require only three Aces so extract only the first three Aces, which should be a Red Ace and two Black Aces. Hand these to the spectator as you come to them and instruct him or her to spread them out in a line face-up. While the spectator is doing this continue to spread the pack until you can see the second Red Ace, which should be very close to the bottom of the face-up pack. If there are only two cards below it close the pack, turn it face down, and place it on the table. If there are more than two cards below it slide the next two cards under the Ace, cut off the cards below those cards, and place them on top of the pack. Then turn the pack face-down and place it on the table. The second Red Ace should now be the third card from the top in the face down pack.

6. There are now three Aces face-up on the table. Pick them up and form them into a face-up pile with the Red Ace on top of the pile.

7. There are now two ways of performing the trick – one using the bridged card and sleights-of-hand, the other not using the bridged card and sleights-of-hand. If you are not using the bridged card and sleights-of-hand proceed directly to paragraph 9 below. If you choose to use the bridged card and sleights-of-hand proceed to paragraph 8 below.

8. In performing the trick you are going to use a handling technique known as a "double lift". (*A description of the handling required is set out in the relevant section of the chapter on "Handling and Sleights-of-Hand".*) Proceed as follows:

   a. Pick up the face-down pack and take the top card, using the handling required for a double lift, *but using only the single top card*. Place this card face-down on the table. Let us assume it is 3S.

   b. Now take what is the top card of the face-up pile of three Aces and hand this Ace (ie. the Red Ace) to the spectator. Instruct him or her to place it face-down on top of the face-down 3S.

   c. Again, using the handling required for a double lift, *but using only a single card*, take the top card of the face-down pack and place this card face-down on top of the face-down Red Ace and the face-down 3S. Let us assume it is 5C.

   d. Now take one of the face-up Black Aces and hand it to the spectator. Instruct him or her to place it face-down on top of the face-down 5C, Red Ace, and 3S. While he or she is doing this prepare a genuine double lift of what is now the top card of the face-down pack (ie. a Red Ace). Perform the double lift, revealing let us assume 2H. Place what the spectator assumes to be 2H (but is, in fact, a Red Ace) face-down on top of the face-down Black Ace, 5C, Red Ace, and 3S. Then instruct the spectator to place the final Black Ace face down on top of these face-down cards.

e. Point out to the spectator that you now have the three face-down Aces placed between the three other cards. Immediately, deal off face-down the top three cards of the face-down packet and instruct the spectator to turn them face-up. They will be three Aces – a Red Ace and two Black Aces.

(NOTE: *The Red Ace is, of course, a different Red Ace to the one the spectator placed face-down on the cards but it is surprising how few spectators will notice this. In any case, even if they do, they will still be mystified as to how that Ace has suddenly appeared. However, you may, if you wish, hide the identity of the second Red Ace. To do this instead of allowing the spectator to turn over the face-down cards pick them up yourself. The Red Ace will be the middle card of the packet and by over-lapping the cards along their length it is possible to display them with only the "A" of the Red Card index being visible.*)

f. Immediately turn the three Aces face-down and place them on top of the three cards you have not dealt out. Point out that this places the three Aces as the top three cards of the packet. Then deal out the cards of the packet face-down onto the table into two 3-card hands, dealing a card to each hand in turn, observing, as you do so, that this will distribute the Aces between the hands. When the deal is finished instruct the spectator to turn the hand to which you dealt first face-up. It will contain three Aces – a Red Ace and two Black Aces. (*Note: This time the Red Ace will be the Red Ace the spectator originally placed on the cards.*)

g. To conclude the trick place the three cards that have not been turned face-up face-down on the face-down pack. (*Note: From the handling at paragraph 4 above the bridged card is the bottom card of the pack.*) You now allow the spectator to place each of the three Aces individually back into the pack either on the top, or the bottom, or in the "middle". As each Ace is placed in the pack the spectator may cut and complete the pack at will – and in each case you cut the pack to take the bridged card to the bottom of the pack. (*For the handling required see the relevant section of the chapter "Handling and Sleights-of-Hand".*)

h. You now tell the spectator that you are going to play a hand of Blind Poker. Explain that what you are going to do is to deal one card to begin: do so, dealing the top card of the pack face-down to the spectator and the second card to yourself. You then explain that you will deal either one or two cards next as the spectator chooses: demonstrate this by first of all dealing off face-down a single card to the spectator and then a single card to yourself, and then dealing off two cards to the spectator and two cards to yourself. This will mean that you then need one card each to make up the Poker hand of five cards: deal off the next card to the spectator and then the next card to yourself.

Immediately pick up the spectator's hand, place it on top of yours and place the combined packet on top of the face-down pack. Then perform a Charlier Shuffle. (*For a description of this shuffle see the relevant section of the chapter "Handling and Sleights-of-Hand".*) After allowing the spectator to cut and complete the pack you cut the bridged card to the bottom of the pack. (*For an explanation of the term "cut and complete" see the "Introduction".*)

i. Now deal the top card of the pack face-down to the spectator and the next card face-down to yourself. Then remind the spectator that he or she may choose to receive either one or two cards. Deal face down to the spectator the number of cards chosen and the same number to yourself. Continue dealing in this way until you both have five cards.

j. Instruct the spectator to turn his or her cards over. He or she may or may not have a good hand, but it is unlikely to be better than yours, which will have three Aces.

9. To perform the trick not using a bridged card and sleights-of-hand proceed as follows:

a. Pick up the face-down pack, take the top card and place it face-down on the table. In doing so, "inadvertently" allow the spectator to glimpse the face of the card.

b. Instruct the spectator to place the Red Ace face-down on top of the card you have just placed on the table. Now take the next card at the top of the pack and place it face-down on top of the two face-down cards on the table, again "inadvertently" allowing the spectator to glimpse the face of the card.

c. Instruct the spectator to place a Black Ace face-down on top of the face-down cards on the table. You then take what is now the top card of the face-down pack (*this time without allowing the spectator to see the face of the card*) and place it face-down on top of the pile of cards on the table. The spectator then adds the second Black Ace face-down to the top of the pile. (*Note: To distract the spectator's attention as you place the top card of the pack on the pile you may, if you wish, at the same time pass the pack to the spectator and ask him or her to shuffle it and place it aside.*)

d. You now continue the trick as described at paragraph 8e and 8f above.

e. To conclude the trick place the three cards that have not been turned face-up face-down onto the face-down pack. In doing so, take the opportunity to note the identity of the bottom card of the pack. Then take the three face-up Aces and place these cards face-down on top of the pack. Having done this perform a Charlier Shuffle. (*For a description of how to do this see the relevant section of the chapter "Handling and Sleights-of-Hand".*) The spectator may now cut-and-complete the pack, at will. (*For an explanation of the term "cut and complete" see the "Introduction".*) When he or she has done so, take the pack, turn it face-up and spread it to show the mix of the cards. In making this spread do not push the cards along the top of the face-up pack – pull the cards along the bottom of the pack using the fingers beneath the pack. Continue with the spread until you see the card you noted the identity of above.

f.   Split the pack at that point and take that card and all the cards below it to what will be the bottom of the face-down pack.

g.   Conclude the trick as described at paragraph 8h, 8i, and 8j above, using the card you identified at paragraph 9e above (which will still be at the bottom of the pack) as a key card. (*For an explanation of how the key card is used see the relevant section in the chapter on "Handling and Sleights-of-Hand".*)

FOURTH TRICK: *"Telepathic Aces"*

1. For this trick you require the two packs of full-sized cards and, if you have one, a Miniature-sized pack, and some rubber bands. However, the trick can be performed with only the two full-sized packs. (*Note: The success of the trick depends upon the cards being in good condition.*)

2. Take the pack you have been using for the previous trick, re-constitute it, and place it face-down on the table. Take the other full-sized pack out of its carton, extract the Joker cards, shuffle it thoroughly, and place it face-down on the table by the side of the other pack.

3. If you are using a Miniature pack take that pack from its carton, extract any Joker cards and any other extraneous cards from it, shuffle it thoroughly, and place it face-down on the table.

4. If you are using a Miniature pack invite the spectator to take that pack, shuffle it, and then to extract from it the two Red Aces. He or she should then shuffle the pack again and insert one of the Red Aces *face-up* anywhere into the face-down pack, leaving it protruding for about half its length. He or she should then insert the other Red Ace (*again face-up*) next to the card either below or above the other Red Ace. The second Red Ace should also protrude from the pack for about half its length. Now, if you have one, place a rubber band around the pack. (*Note: You now have a card in the Miniature pack sandwiched between two Red Aces.*) Take the pack in

your right hand with the face of the cards towards you and the faces of the reversed Aces towards the spectator, carefully covering the base of the pack and the area below it with the back of the hand. Your thumb should be across the face of the card facing you, about ¾ of the way down the pack. Your first finger should be at the bottom inner corner with the other three fingers below the level of the bottom end of the pack. If you wish, you may place the index and second finger of the left hand over the index and second finger of the right hand with the other two fingers of the left hand below the level of the little finger of the right hand.

5. You now instruct the spectator to push the two Aces together into the pack. (*This action will "pump-push" the card between the two Aces out at the bottom of the pack.*) Note the identity of this card (*which is covered from the view of the spectators by the back of the right hand*) and, while the spectator is handing you the Miniature pack carton, push this card back into the pack.

6. You then hand the pack to the spectator, who places it into its carton, which is then placed aside.

7. If you are not using a Miniature pack go through exactly the same procedure as described in paragraphs 4, 5, and 6 above with one of the full-sized packs.

8. Now take one of the full-sized packs (or, if you are not using a Miniature pack, the remaining full-sized pack), turn it face up and go through it to extract the two Red Aces. In fact, what you are also doing is locating the card you noted at paragraph 5 above. When you do locate the card, you should cut the pack to place this card as the bottom card of the face-down pack.

9. The spectator now places one of the Red Aces face-up either on the top or at the bottom of the pack as he or she wishes, and then cuts and completes the pack, at will. (*For an explanation of the term "cut and complete" see the "Introduction".*) Finally, you instruct the spectator to go through the face-down pack, locate the face-up Ace, and to then place the second Red Ace face-up on top of the first face-down card above the first Red Ace. You then take the pack and, if you have one, place a rubber band around it before placing it in its appropriate carton.

10. If you are not using a Miniature pack proceed directly to paragraph 12 below. If you are using a Miniature pack now take the remaining full-sized pack and repeat the procedure described in paragraph 8 above. Then take one of the Red Aces and place it face-up on top of the face-down pack, the Ace projecting forward from the pack by about half its length. You then cut and complete the pack to take the projecting Ace to about the centre of the pack. Now spread the face-down pack to allow the spectator to place the other Red Ace (face-up) on top of the first face-down card above the first red Ace. If you have one, now place a rubber band around the pack. In any case, return the pack to its appropriate carton with the two Red Aces projecting from the carton end. (*For a definition of "cut and complete" see the "Introduction".*)

11. As you have been using a Miniature pack you should proceed as follows:

    a. Instruct the spectator to take the Miniature pack out of its carton, to remove the rubber band (if used), and to identify the card between the two Aces.

b. Next instruct the spectator take the first full-sized pack used out of its carton, to remove the rubber band (if used), and to identify the card between the two Aces.

c. The spectator should then take the second full-sized pack used and push the projecting Aces into the carton. He or she then removes the pack from the carton, removes the rubber band (if used), and identifies the card between the two Aces.

d. All the cards between the two Aces should be identical.

12. As you have not been using a Miniature pack you should proceed as follows:

a. Instruct the spectator to take the first full-sized pack used out of its carton, to remove the rubber band (if used) and to identify the card between the two Aces.

b. The spectator should then repeat this process with the second full-sized pack.

c. The cards between the two Aces should be identical.

Fifth Trick: *"Just Think of An Ace"*

1. Allow the spectator to choose any of the two full-sized packs and to extract the four Aces from it. You then take the Aces and place them face-up on the table in a fan formation with the AC at the bottom of the fan, the AH on top of it, the AS next, and the AD as the top card of the face-up fan. (NOTE: *Useful mnemonics that could help you to remember the order are:* $C - H - a - S - e - D$ *or the phrase "Curly Hair Settles Down".)*

2. Pick up the remainder of the pack and shuffle it. Then allow the spectator to shuffle it.

3. If you are performing the routine not using sleights-of-hand and a bridged card proceed directly to paragraph 9. If you are using sleights-of-hand and a bridged card proceed directly to the next paragraph.

4. Instruct the spectator to think of any one of the Aces. Collect the Aces together and turn them face-down. (*They are now from the top AC, AH, AS, and AD.*)

5. Take each Ace separately off the pile and place it in the "middle" of the pack under the control of the bridged card, which each time you cut to the bottom of the pack. (*For an explanation of how to use the bridged card in this way see the relevant sections in the chapter on "Handling and Sleights-of-Hand".*) On the final cut of the bridged card to the bottom of the pack the cards at the top of the face-down pack are in the order AD, AS, AH, and AC. The spectator may now cut and

complete the pack at will – provided that, finally, you cut the bridged card to the bottom of the pack. (*For an explanation of the term "cut and complete" see the "Introduction".*)

6. Now deal of the top 13 cards of the face-down pack into a face-down pile (Pile A), then the next 13 cards into a second face-down pile (Pile B), then the next 13 cards into a third face-down pile (Pile C), and then place the next and final 13 cards on the table *without dealing them out* (Pile D). (*Note: The Aces are now at the bottom of Pile A and the bridged card is at the bottom of Pile D.*)

7. Your aim now is to produce a face-down pack with Pile A at the top of the pack. This can be achieved as follows:

    a. Allow the spectator a free choice of any two piles which are then combined – as are the other two piles. However, in the case of Pile A and Pile D, the Pile D goes on top of Pile A; in other combinations Pile A goes on top and Pile D on the bottom.

    b. The spectator may then place any combined pair on the top or bottom of any other combined pair. He or she may then cut and complete the pack, at will.

    c. If you then cut the bridged card to the bottom of the pack Pile A will be at the top of the pack.

8. The pack is now configured to allow the spectator's thought-of-Ace to be spelled out as follows:

    a. "A-C-E-O-F-C-L-U-B-S"

Take a card off the top of the pack for each letter. AC is the card at the "S" of the spelling.

b. "A-C-E-O-F-H-E-A-R-T-S"
    The AH is at the "S" of the spelling.

c. "A-C-E-O-F-S-P-A-D-E-S"
    AS is the *next card in the pack*, ie. the top card of the pack after the spelling out of the card.

d. "A-C-E-O-F-D-I-A-M-O-N-D-S"
    AD is at the "S" of the spelling.

9. As you are not using sleights-of-hand and a bridged card to perform the routine you will need to employ a subterfuge to control the cards. This is provided for in the handling set out in the following paragraphs.

10. The position is that there are four face-up Aces in a fan on the table and you have the remaining 48 cards of the pack. Deal out these 48 cards into four face-down piles of 12 cards each and invite the spectator to turn the face-up fan of Aces face-down and place it on top of any one of the piles. Instruct him or her to then think of and remember any one of the Aces. Then he or she should place any one of the other three piles on top of the pile on which he or she has placed the Aces. The other two piles are put aside.

11. You now take the combined pile of face-down cards containing the Aces and mix it as follows:

    a. From the top of the pack deal four cards face-down in a pile on the table. Then from the bottom deal off face-down onto the pile four cards. Continue this process of dealing alternately from the top and then the bottom of the block of cards until you have only four cards left – deal these onto the top of the face-down pile.

b. Pick up the pile and as you do so note the bottom card of the packet. Now perform a Charlier Shuffle. (*For a description of how this is done see the relevant section of the chapter "Handling and Sleights-of-Hand".*) When the shuffle has been completed turn the packet face-up and spread it to show the mix of the cards. In performing this spread move the cards from the bottom of the packet from right to left, each card sliding above the preceding card. Continue with the spread until you locate the card you noted above. Cut the spread at that point so as to place the noted card at the bottom card of the face-down pack.

12. Immediately deal off face-down onto the table the top 13 cards of the packet. Keep what is left of the packet in your hand. Now ask the spectator: "Which of the packets do you want?" If the spectator chooses the pile you have dealt out onto the table discard the cards you have in your hand. If he or she chooses the cards you have in your hand give them to him or her and immediately pick up the pile on the table.

13. Having picked up the pile from the table ask the spectator to name his or her thought-of Ace. You proceed to spell out the Ace using the spelling system set out at paragraph 8 above. As you spell out the thought-of Ace you should place the cards as they are being removed to the bottom of the packet.

Sixth Trick: *"All Together Now"*

1. This trick is performed using the two full-sized packs. Re-constitute them, extract the Aces and then shuffle them. Then place the two packs side by side.

2. Invite the spectator to cut off about half of each pack and to place these cards aside. You take the cards that are left and riffle shuffle them into each other. Having done so you place the combined packet *face-up* on the table. (*For an explanation of the term "riffle shuffle" see the relevant sections in the chapter on "Handling and Sleights-of-Hand".*)

3. The spectator is now asked to turn the Aces *face-down* and to insert them individually into the packet. You then take the packet, cut it roughly in half, and riffle shuffle one half into the other half. You then cut the shuffled packet roughly in half and place the top half (Pile A) to your left and the bottom half (Pile B) to your right. In placing Pile B on the table turn it over without drawing attention to this move.

4. Now cut off about half of the cards from the top of Pile A and place them by the side of Pile B. In doing so, make it quite clear that you are turning them over. Do the same with Pile B, placing the cards by the side of Pile A.

5. Invite the spectator to shuffle the cards by the side of Pile A into that pile, while you riffle shuffle the cards by the side of Pile B into that pile.

6. Now repeat paragraphs 4 and 5 at least one more time. After the final repetition, in placing Pile B on the table turn it over – again without drawing attention to this move.

7. Now take the two piles and riffle shuffle them into each other. (*Note: The eight Aces should now be face-down in the packet of otherwise face-up cards.*)

8. Hand the packet (face-up) to the spectator, instructing him or her to go through it and to extract any face-down cards, placing each face-down card face-down in a pile on the table according to the colour of its back. He or she should end the sorting out of the packet with a pile of four cards of one colour back and four cards of the other colour back. When the piles are turned face-up each will contain the four Aces of the relevant pack.

ADAPTATIONS AND ALTERNATIVES

.THE CONTEXT IN WHICH card magic is performed largely determines the tricks that can be used and the effects that can be achieved. The performer who plies his trade in the theatre is likely to use a larger-than-life style of presentation with tricks that appeal more by the strength of their outcomes rather than any direct involvement of the audience. He or she may also be able to achieve effects by manipulations and sleights-of-hand that would be fool-hardy if performed in close proximity to the spectators. However, most performers present their tricks to a small number of people – usually in a social group seated around a table. In these circumstances he or she should attempt with each trick to involve all the spectators. In this way not only is their interest in the performance enhanced but their direct involvement distracts their attention from the mechanics of the trick. In other words they are more concerned with what is being done rather than how it is being done. In addition, in such a setting attempts to deceive the spectators by intricate handling or by complex sleights-of-hand are unlikely to be successful. Ideally, what is required are self-working tricks with a minimum of manipulation.

The tricks described in the preceding chapter, "*The Routine*", meet most of these criteria for performance before a small audience. The one requirement they do not meet is the total involvement of the audience if that audience is more than one spectator. However, the tricks are easily adapted to involve additional spectators. For example, in the first trick, "*Finding The Aces*", three spectators could be involved – one for each of the Aces to be found from the pack. A fourth spectator could be involved if the three spectators handed their cards face-down to that spectator to whom you also handed the fourth and final Ace. Alternatively, the first three spectators could retain their face-down cards and, after you have handed the final face-down card to the fourth spectator, they could all turn their cards face-up to reveal the Aces. Similarly, in the second, fourth, and sixth tricks ("*You Must Be Joking*", "*Telepathic Aces*", *and* "*All Together Now*") there are a number of occasions in the course of the presentation when a second, third, or even fourth spectator could be invited to perform whatever procedure is required at that point.

The third trick, "*Chard Sharper's Aces*", is very much a presentation by the performer – although even with this trick it would be possible to involve three spectators, each placing an Ace in turn onto the pile before the deal is made. However, if this was done, it would be necessary to ensure that the cards were distributed to the spectators in such a way that the Aces were placed in the appropriate order.

The fifth trick, "*Just Think of An Ace*", could be adapted to involve up to four spectators, but great care would need to be taken to prevent such an adaptation revealing how the effect was being achieved. Probably the safest way of adapting the trick is to proceed as follows:

a. Invite each of up to four spectators to think of an Ace.

b. Allow different spectators to choose how the piles are combined.

c. In spelling out the thought-of Aces, take the cards off the top of the packet without disturbing their order and, after the Ace has been revealed, place it back face-down on top of the pack. Then place all the other cards face-down on top of the face-down pack.

d. Use a bridged card or a key card to allow the packet to be cut and completed after the return of the cards to the pack. *(For an explanation of how to use a bridged card or a key card see the relevant sections in the chapter on "Handling and Sleights-of-Hand".)*

For those readers who do not wish to adapt the tricks in this way alternative or additional tricks are described below – each designed to involve a specific number of spectators:

a. *"Magic Clocks"* – two spectators.

b. *"Spell Them Out"* – three spectators.

c. *"More Aces"* – four spectators.

d. *"Everybody's Ace"* – any number of spectators

"Magic Clocks"
(For Two Spectators)

1. For this trick you require two packs of cards – say one Blue-backed and the other Red-backed. Take the Blue-backed pack, hand it to the first spectator and invite him or her to give it a thorough shuffle. Do the same using the Red-backed pack with the second spectator.

2. Take the Blue-backed pack from the first spectator and turn it face-up. You now spread out the pack to show the mix of the cards. You perform this spread with both hands (palms up) beneath the pack with the thumbs on the face of the cards. The spread is made by moving the cards from right to left (*from your point of view*) using the right thumb, ie. the cards are spread moving each card underneath the preceding card. When you come to an Ace (preferably about the middle of the pack) draw this Ace under the left-hand cards using the fingers of the left hand. Continue to spread the cards using the right thumb but exert sufficient pressure on the left-hand of the spread to prevent any further cards being forced underneath the selected Ace. When the spread is completed separate the pack at the point at which the selected Ace is the bottom card of the left-hand spread. Split the pack at this point, moving the right-hand packet to the right, and then place this packet on top of the left-hand packet. Now turn the pack face-down and place it on the table. (*Note: If the procedure described*

above has been correctly performed the selected Ace is now the top card of the face-down pack.)

3. Repeat the procedure using the Red-backed pack, placing the identical Ace to the top of the face-down pack. If on the initial spread of the face-up cards the identical Ace is not conveniently positioned cut the pack to place it at a convenient point and spread the cards again.

4. Now deal from the top of the face-down packs 12 cards of the Blue-backed pack in front of the first spectator and the top 12 cards of the Red-backed pack in front of the second spectator. As you do so explain to them that you want each of them to cut off a packet of cards from the top of their face-down piles. Also explain to them that neither you nor they should know how many cards they have cut off. Suggest that they should immediately put them into a pocket or sit on them.

5. When this has been done place the remaining cards of each pile (without disturbing their order) face-down on top of the appropriate face-down pack. As you pick up each pack to replace the cards secretly note the identity of the bottom card of each pack.

6. Each pack is then placed face-down on the table and the spectators are invited to cut and complete their packs, at will. (*For an explanation of the term "cut and complete" see the "Introduction".*) When this has been done take each pack, turn it face-up, and spread it to show the mix of the cards. In doing so, locate the card in each pack that you noted at paragraph 5 above and cut the pack to place this card at the bottom card of the face-down pack.

7. For each face-down pack now deal out the top 12 cards onto the table in the form of a clock. In placing the cards you should begin at the 11 o'clock position and then place the cards anti-clockwise, ie., 10 o'clock, 9 o'clock, 8 o'clock etc. The 12th and final card for each pack is placed in the 12 o'clock position.

8. Invite each spectator to take the cards he or she cut off at paragraph 4 above and to count them. When they have done this instruct them to take the card in the appropriate clock at the hour corresponding to the number of cards they cut off. They should place the two cards face-down side by side.

9. Now instruct them to turn the cards face-up. When they do so they will find that they have arrived at identical Aces.

"Spell Them Out"
(*For Three Spectators*)

1. For this trick you require two packs of cards – say, one Blue-backed and the other Red-backed. Both packs are separately and thoroughly shuffled. The spectators then select one of the packs. You split this pack roughly into three equal packets and hand a packet to each of the three spectators, instructing them to extract the Aces and to place the remaining cards aside. While they are doing this you "play" with the other pack and, as you are doing so, you place the Aces of that pack face-down on top of the pack. The order in which the Aces are placed is immaterial.

2. Take the Aces the spectators have separated out from their pack, say the Red-backed pack. Extract AD and place it face-up in front of yourself. Then take the other three Aces, turn them face-down, mix them, and allow each spectator to choose a card, which they should place face-down in front of themselves. The remaining Red-backed cards are placed aside.

3. Now place the Blue-backed pack face-down in front of the first spectator and instruct him or her to cut off about the top $\frac{1}{3}$ of the pack and to deal the cards he or she has cut off into four piles, dealing a card to each pile in turn. Instruct the second spectator to cut off about half of what is left of the pack and do the same, continuing to deal them from the point at which the first spectator finished his or her deal. The third spectator is then

invited to take the remaining cards of the Blue-backed pack and to continue the deal from the point at which the second spectator finished his or her deal. When the dealing has been completed, consolidate the pack by picking up the piles in any order as determined by the spectators.

4. Having done so you instruct the first spectator to place his or her card face-down on top of the pack and to cut and complete the pack. You then perform a Charlier Shuffle, after which you invite the spectator to cut and complete the pack again. Once he or she has done so, go through the pack to locate the Red-backed card and cut the pack to place this card as the top card of the face-down pack. Then turn it face-up to reveal its identity. (*For an explanation of the term "cut and complete" see the "Introduction" and for a description of the Charlier Shuffle see the chapter "Handling and Sleights-of-Hand".*)

5. You now proceed to spell out the identity of the Ace, using the following system of spelling:

   a. "T-H-E-A-C-E-O-F H-E-A-R-T-S", "T-H-E-A-C-E-O-F S-P-A-D-E-S", etc., as appropriate, taking the face-up card as the first letter of the spelling, moving each card to the hand not holding the pack, and placing each card under the preceding card.

   b. If you are spelling out AH or AS when you come to the "S" of the spelling leave that card face-down on the pack, place the pack on the table, turn the face-up card of the counted-out packet face-down and place it in front of yourself. Then place the Blue-backed cards of the packet aside. Now pick up the pack, take the top card, and place it face-down somewhere in the middle of the table.

c. If you are spelling out AC, when you come to the "S" of the spelling you take *all* the cards of the spelling into the hand not holding the pack before placing the pack on the table. You then proceed as in paragraph 5b above.

6. You now repeat the whole procedure as described in paragraphs 4 and 5 above for the second and then the third spectator.

7. The situation you have now arrived at is that there are three face-down Blue-backed cards in the middle of the table and the remaining cards of the Blue-backed pack face-down on the table. In front of you are three face-down Red-backed cards and a face-up Red-backed AD.

8. Point out that only AD remains. Pick it up and place it face-down on top of the other three Red-backed cards. Then place all four Red-backed cards on top of the remaining cards of the Blue-backed pack. Pick up this packet and turn the top card face-up (ie. AD) and proceed to spell out "T-H-E-A-C-E-O-F D-I-A-M-O-N-D-S" using the spelling procedure described at paragraph 5a. above. However, in this case do not transfer the cards from the pack to the hand not holding the pack. Instead transfer each card as it is spelled out to the bottom of the packet of cards. When the spelling is completed there will be a face-down Blue-backed card at the top of the packet.

9. Take this card from the top of the packet and place it face-down with the other three face-down cards in the

middle of the table. Underneath it will be a face-up AD, turn it face-down and place it with the four face-down Blue-backed cards in the middle of the table. The next three cards in the packet will be the three Red-backed cards, place these three cards with the other face-down cards in the middle of the table and place the remaining Blue-backed cards of the packet aside.

10. Now pick up all the face-down cards in the middle of the table and deal them out into a face-up pile. You will deal out eight Aces.

"More Aces"
(*For Four Spectators*)

1. Ideally this trick follows one in which two packs have
    been used. This will allow you to invite the spectator to
    reconstitute one of the packs and return it to its carton
    while you reconstitute the other pack. As you are doing
    so you should secretly place the four Aces face-down on
    top of the face-down pack (and, if you are using it, the
    bridged card at the bottom of the pack).

2. If you are not using a bridged card proceed directly to
    paragraph 4. If you are using a bridged card proceed
    directly to the next paragraph. (*For an explanation of the
    term "bridged card" see the "Introduction" and the chapter
    on "Handling and Sleights-of-Hand".*)

3. False mix the pack using the handling described in the
    relevant section of the chapter "*Handling and Sleights-
    of-Hand*".

4. Turn the pack face up and spread it out to show the mix
    of the pack. As you do this take care not to display the
    Aces which will be the bottom four cards of the face-up
    pack.

5. Place the pack face-down on the table and invite a
    spectator to cut it into four roughly equal face-down
    piles in the following manner: he or she first of all cuts
    off about the top ¾ of the pack, leaving Pile A (what was
    the bottom of the pack), they then cut off about ¾ of
    the rest of the pack, leaving Pile B, then the top half of

the remainder of the pack, leaving Pile C. The packet that remains (what was the top of the pack) is Pile D.

6. Pile A is placed in front of the first spectator, Pile B in front of the second spectator, Pile C in front of the third spectator, and Pile D in front of the fourth spectator.

7. The first spectator now takes Pile A and deals a card from it face-down in front of the other three piles and then places his or her remaining cards face-down in front of him- or herself. Each of the three piles is then placed face-down on top of the card in front of it. The first spectator then takes Pile A again and deals a card from the top of it face-down onto the top of the three piles. He or she then places the remaining cards face-down in front of him- or herself.

8. The second spectator now takes Pile B and repeats the procedure described in paragraph 7 above. The third spectator does the same with Pile C, and, finally, the fourth spectator does the same with Pile D. (*Note: The Aces are now the top cards of each of the piles and the trick could be brought to a satisfactory conclusion at this point. However, a much stronger finish can be produced by continuing as described below.*)

9. Instruct the first spectator to cut off from the top of his or her face-down pile about half the cards and to place them face-down by the side of the remaining cards. You take the remaining cards, turn them face-up, and place them across the face-down cards to form a cross.

10. Now turn to the second spectator. Pick up his or her face-down cards and count the number of cards in the packet without reversing their order (*see the "Introduction" for an explanation of how this is done*). You then invite the

spectator to think of and state any number below this total number of cards. When he or she has done so, count the number of cards corresponding to the stated number off the top of the face-down packet *without reversing their order*. Place the cards you have counted off face-down on the table, turn the remaining cards face-up, and place them across the face-down cards to form a cross.

11. Turn now to the third spectator. Instruct him or her to cut off as many cards as he or she wishes from their face-down pile and to turn them face-up. You then take the face-down cards and place them on top of the face-up cards - then turn the packet over. The spectator again cuts off as many cards as he or she wishes from the top of the packet and turns them over. You place the remaining cards of the packet on top of them – and then turn the whole packet over. You then instruct the spectator to take the first face-up card from the top of the packet and to place it across the top of the packet to form a cross.

12. Finally, invite the fourth spectator to deal off face-down onto the table as many cards as he or she wishes from the top of his or her packet. When this has been done place the undealt cards aside. Then instruct the spectator to deal the cards he or she has counted out into two face-down piles. Note the pile to which the last card is dealt: this pile will have the Ace as its top card. Now invite the spectator to place one of the piles on top of the cards you put aside. If the spectator places the pile with the Ace on top of the other cards then instruct him or her to place all these cards on top of the pile he or she has retained.

If the spectator places the pile without the Ace on top of the other cards then instruct him or her to place the pile he or she has retained on top of the other cards. In either case, the pile with the Ace becomes the top cards of the combined packet. The spectator is now invited to take the top card of the packet and to place it across the top of the packet to form a cross.

13. You now have the fourth spectator's packet with a single face-down card across the top of it and the other three spectators' packets with face-up cards across the top of face-down cards.

14. Instruct the first, second, and third spectators to remove the face-up cards from their piles and to turn over the first face-down card. They will all be Aces.

15. Finally, instruct the fourth spectator to turn over the face down card on top of his or her packet. It will be the fourth Ace.

"Everybody's Ace"
(*For Any Number of Spectators*)

1. Each spectator involved is handed the pack of cards and instructed to shuffle it.

2. You take back the pack from the last spectator involved, shuffle it, and spread it face-up to show the mix of the cards. In doing so, note the position of a conveniently placed Ace and cut the cards at the point that places this Ace as the top card of the face-down pack.

3. Place the pack face-down on the table and instruct the first spectator to take the top card. Instruct him or her to note it secretly without revealing it to either you or to any of the other spectators. When he or she has done so instruct him or her to place the card face-down on top of the face-down pack.

4. A second spectator is instructed to cut off about half of the pack, which he or she should place face-down on the table. Now instruct the spectator to take the bottom part of the packet, to turn it face-up, and to place it on top of the packet he or she has just cut off. Finally, you instruct him or her to turn over the whole packet. You then take the pack and cut it exactly in the same way, including the final turning over of the whole packet. (*Note: When you make your cut you should ensure that you are cutting below the level at which the spectator cut.*) When you have completed the whole procedure you place the pack in front of the spectator and instruct him

or her to take the first face-down card in the pack. He
or she should note the card secretly without revealing it
to either you or to any of the other spectators. When the
spectator has done this, instruct him or her to place the
card face-down on the table, to turn any face-up cards
in the pack face-down, and *to place the face-down pack
on top of it.*

5. You now take the face-down pack, cut off about the top
    ¾ of the cards, turn these cards over, and place them at
    the bottom of the pack. You then turn the pack over, cut
    off about the top ½ of the cards, turn these cards over and
    place them at the bottom of the pack. You then turn the
    whole pack over and spread it until you locate the first
    face-up card. You cut the pack at this point leaving the
    face-down card above the face-up card in place. The other
    face-down cards above that card you turn over and place
    at the bottom of the pack. You then place the pack on the
    table and instruct the third spectator to take the top card
    of the pack and to note it secretly without revealing it to
    either you or the other spectators. When the spectator has
    done this instruct him or her to place the card on top of
    the pack. Then go through the pack and turn any face-
    up cards face-down. Having done this, place the pack
    face-down on the table.

6. Immediately turn to the fourth spectator and, as you
    do, pick up the pack and begin dealing cards from
    the top of the pack face-down in a pile on the table,
    counting them mentally as you do. Once you have
    passed 20 instruct the spectator to stop you dealing at
    whatever point he or she wishes. When he or she has
    done so, stop the deal at that point, and instruct him
    or her to cut off from the top of the pile as many cards
    as he or she wishes and immediately either put them

in a pocket or hide them away. Point out that this is because you do not want to know how many cards have been taken nor do you want him or her to know. When this has been done begin dealing out cards again onto the pile and again ask the spectator to stop the deal at any point. When he or she has done so ask him or her again to cut off any number of cards from the top of the pile and again to hide them away. Now take the cards remaining on the pile and place them on top of the remaining cards of the pack – as you do this (or at some convenient time before) note the identity of the bottom card of the pack. Now perform a Charlier Shuffle of the face-down pack. Then turn the pack face-up and perform a second Charlier Shuffle. As you do, spread the blocks of cards as you take them from the pack so that you are able to locate the card you identified above. When you do so place that block (with the identified card as its face card) as the top block of the face-up pack, which will result in that card being the bottom card of the face-down pack. *(For an explanation of how to perform a Charlier Shuffle see the relevant section of the chapter on "Handling and Sleights-of-Hand".)* Now immediately deal out into a face-down pile on the table a number of cards equal to the cards previously dealt out in the first and second deal. You do this without counting out aloud or stating the number. You then instruct the spectator to take the cards he or she has cut off and hidden and to count them. While the spectator is counting his or her cards pick up the pile you have dealt onto the table and place it on top of the pack. You then count off from the top of the pack the number of cards corresponding to the number arrived at by the spectator, transferring them to the bottom of the pack. The spectator is then instructed to take the top card of the pack, to note it secretly, and not to reveal it either to you or any other spectator. He or she should then place the card face-down on top of the pack.

7. If more than four spectators are to be involved in the trick you should go through the sequence of procedures described in paragraphs 4, 5, and 6 above again to the point at which all the spectators have taken and noted a card. The final spectator to take a card should replace it on the top of the face-down pack.

8. In handling the pack after the replacement of this card by the last spectator note the identify of the bottom card of the pack. Having done so, allow each of the spectators who are taking part in the trick to cut and complete *(For an explanation of the term "cut and complete" see the "Introduction".)* You then take the pack, turn it face-up and spread it show the mix of the cards. Note the location of your noted card and cut the pack to place this card at the bottom of the face-down pack.

9. With the pack face-down now deal out face-down onto the table as many cards as there are spectators who have taken and noted a card. Having done so, pick up the cards you have dealt out and mix them. Then, with the cards still face-down to you, hand the packet to each spectator in turn and ask them to confirm that their card is in the packet.

10. You now take the packet and spread it out face-up on the table. You instruct the spectators on your count of "1-2-3" to shout out the identity of their card and to pick it up. They will all shout out and attempt to pick up the same Ace.

HANDLING AND
SLEIGHTS-OF-HAND

THIS CHAPTER, WHICH DEALS with the techniques that can be used to manipulate and control the cards, is for the most part reproduced from the companion volume to this book: "*Old Wine In A New Bottle*". Some amendments have been made to the handling in some of the manipulations and some additional material has been added (eg. The Double Lift).

It is not intended that the newcomer to card magic should work methodically through the material studying and practising each technique. Such a procedure would not only be counter-productive but also boring in the extreme. Rather what is intended is that the reader should use the chapter as a reference source on the various techniques, turning to it as required during the study of the various tricks and for this reason extensive references are made to this chapter in the descriptions of the performance of the tricks. However, the beginner is strongly advised to master at the very outcome a number of essential skills. These are:

The Overhand Shuffle and Controls
The Riffle Shuffle and Controls
A False Shuffle
A False Cut

With regard to the use of the techniques a word of warning is appropriate: do not over-use them. They do allow you to create the illusion of the cards being indiscriminately mixed. They do allow you to place cards in positions in a pack or packet that facilitate an effect. However, if they are used when they are not essential (either as a habit or to give you a degree of personal satisfaction in deluding the audience) their very use will give rise to suspicion and the spectators, seeing the moves used so often, will begin to look carefully at them and thus might detect the subterfuge involved.

Practice the techniques to the point at which they are almost automatic in performance and do not look at your hands when performing them. If you look at your hands the chances are that the spectators will too and what would go unobserved will be closely examined.

THE OVERHAND SHUFFLE

Hold the pack face-down, with the outer end towards the spectators. The cards' outer sides should rest on the part of the palm at the junction between the palm and the fingers at an angle of about 45°, the inner side upward. The thumb rests across the top card of the pack, and the first finger is against the outer corner. The other fingers rest on the face of the bottom card.

Using the hand not holding the pack lift up the bottom half or so of the pack with the thumb holding the inner end of the packet and the first three fingers at the outer end.

Move the packet over the top of the other packet and pull off from the top of it single cards or clumps of cards with the thumb of the hand holding what was the top part of the pack, allowing the cards or single card to fall onto that packet as the packet in the other hand is moved backwards and forwards.

Carry on with this procedure until all the cards have been pulled off what was the bottom of the pack onto what was the top of the pack.

To continue the shuffle, again cut away the bottom half or so of the pack and go through the procedure gain.

CONTROLLING THE CARDS

The top card can be taken to the bottom of the pack by slipping the card off the top of the pack as the shuffle begins and immediately shuffling off the rest of the pack onto it, ie. the whole pack other than the top card is lifted to begin the shuffle.

The bottom card of the pack can be moved to the top of the pack by beginning the shuffle by lifting about the bottom $^2/_3$ of the pack. This packet is held between the thumb at the inner end and the second and third fingers at the outer end. As the shuffle progresses pressure is exerted on the final card in the packet to ensure that it is the final card shuffled off.

To hold the bottom card at the bottom of the pack the shuffle begins by lifting the packet which will be shuffled off from the middle of the pack and allowing the top and bottom remaining packets to fall together.

To transpose the top and bottom cards of the pack begin by slipping the top card as described above for taking the top card to the bottom. Then shuffle off all the other cards onto it exerting pressure on the final card (what was the bottom card of the pack) to ensure that this card is the final card shuffled off.

THE RIFFLE SHUFFLE

Hold the pack face-down with the outer side of the pack towards the spectators. The pack is held with both hands, the thumbs at the inner side and the fingers at the outer side.

Split the pack into two halves, moving the top half to the left and the bottom half to the right, and place the two halves face-down on the table end to end, the outer sides of the packets still towards the spectators.

Move the two packets against each other until the two inner corners are touching and form the point a V with the open end of the V facing the spectators.

Change the position of the hands holding the packets so that the thumbs are immediately behind the corners forming the point of the V, the little fingers at the corners of the outside ends, the first fingers pressing down on the packets at the open part of the V. The little fingers are pushing at the end outside corners. The other fingers are at the outer sides of the packets.

Push down with all the fingers and at the same time lift the inner sides off the table with the thumbs, keeping the two corners forming the sharp end of the V in close contact.

Allow the cards to fall away in a cascade from the bottom of each packet interleaving with each other as they fall.

Close the V by pushing the inner ends of the two packets together thus completely inter-weaving them.

Push the two packets into each other and square up the pack.

CONTROLLING THE CARDS

To retain the top card or a top block of cards at the top of the shuffled pack control the release of the left hand packet (ie. what was the top half of the pack) so that the desired card or cards drop last.

To retain the bottom card or a bottom block of cards at the bottom of the shuffled pack allow the bottom card or the bottom cards of the right hand packet (ie. what was the bottom half of the pack) to fall first.

THE CHARLIER SHUFFLE

With the outer ends of the cards facing the spectators, the pack is placed face-down diagonally across the up-turned palm immediately adjoining the base of the fingers. The thumb is at the outer side of the pack towards the outer corner and the tips of the fingers curl around the inner side.

The basic shuffle (or, rather, mix) begins by the other hand (palm down) moving over the pack. The thumb of this hand is at the inner end of the pack with the top of the third finger curling over the outer end towards the inner corner. The pack is then tilted, the outer side of the pack pivoting on the upturned palm of the up-turned hand.

The upper hand now slides out a small packet of cards from the **bottom** of the pack, leaving the remainder of the pack resting on the fingers of the lower hand, the thumb of which moves onto the top of the pack.

This thumb now pushes off a small packet of cards from the **top** of what was the pack and these cards are slid **beneath** the cards held in the other (down-turned) hand.

The fingers of the up-turned hand now push off a small packet of cards from the **bottom** of what was the pack and these cards are placed on the **top** of the cards in the other (down-turned) hand.

This alternating top and bottom extraction of cards is continued until all the cards that constituted the original pack have been transferred and the shuffle (or mix) is complete. The rule to be remembered is that cards taken from the bottom go on top, and cards taken from the top go to the bottom.

CONTROLLING THE CARDS

Although the cards appear to have been thoroughly mixed the outcome of the shuffle is the same as would have resulted if the pack had been cut and completed. So, if at the end of the shuffle you cut the original bottom card of the pack back to the bottom of the pack then the pack will be back in its original order. Alternatively, if you had started with a bridged card at the bottom of the pack and if you cut it back to the bottom of the pack after the shuffle you would restore the pack to its original order.

Another method of controlling the mix when using a small packet of cards is to note the number of cards being transferred during the mix and then to perform a second mix transferring the same sequence of cards but this time starting the mix from the top of the pack. For example, if on the first mix of a 12-card packet you take four cards off the bottom, three off the top, two off the bottom, leaving three cards to be placed at the bottom and you then on the second mix take four cards off the top, three of the bottom, two off the top, leaving three cards to be placed on the top, the pack will be back in its original order. It might be thought that such handling would be immediately noted by the spectators but if it is done boldly and quickly it will be accepted as a fair mix of the pack.

CREATING AND HANDLING A BRIDGED CARD

There are a number of ways in which the bottom card of the pack may be handled to produce a convex bridge.

For the first, hold the pack face down with the outer end towards the spectators. The thumb is positioned on the outer side and the fingers wrap around the inner side. Move the other hand over the pack, the thumb at the inner end of the pack and the fingers at the outer end, and lift the pack very slightly, allowing the bottom card to fall onto and rest on the palm of the hand originally holding the pack, the separation of the card being facilitated by a slight upward pressure by the thumb of the upper hand on the rest of the pack, and the procedure being concealed by tilting the pack, ie. raising the inner end. Squeeze the card at its sides using the fingers of the lower hand to press the card against the fleshy part of the palm at the base of the thumb of the same hand. Only very slight pressure to produce a very slight bridge is required. Then allow the pack to drop back onto the card. The bottom card is bridged along its length with a convex bridge.

For the second, again hold the pack face-down with the outer end towards the spectators. The pack rests on the palm of the hand with the thumb at the outer side and the fingers wrapped around the inner side. The other hand moves over the pack and lifts it leaving the bottom card in the palm of the hand originally holding the pack. The pack is then turned so that the inner side points downwards towards the single card. The cards are then allowed to fall in a cascade onto the single card which is held between the fingers and thumbs of the lower hand. This will produce a "round of applause" (ie. the sound of cards falling onto the single card). More significantly, it produces a convex bridge of the card along its length.

A third method, which again allows you to bridge the card quite openly without raising any suspicion in the spectators, is to play with the pack in a very casual way while you are chatting with them. In doing so order the cards so that the card you wish to bridge is either the top card or bottom card of the face-down pack. When this has been achieved suddenly cut the pack into two roughly equal packets and hand the packet not containing the card you wish to bridge to a spectator, instructing him or her to shuffle it. While he or she is doing so you shuffle the packet you have retained to either take the top card to the bottom or the bottom card to the top and then back to the bottom, depending upon the initial position of the card you wish to bridge. At this point the spectator is likely to have completed his or her shuffle. Ask him or her to either give the packet another good shuffle or, if there is more than one spectator, to pass it to another spectator for them to shuffle. As this is being done turn your packet face-up and, while playing with the cards as you watch and chat with the spectator/s, take the top face-up card and, under cover of the hand not holding the packet, give that card a convex bridge along its length. Once you have done this cut the packet to place the bridged card roughly in the middle of the packet and turn the packet face-down. Now exchange packets with the spectator/s, instructing them to shuffle the second packet while you shuffle the other packet. The two packets are then placed together to reconstitute the pack (with somewhere within it your bridged card).

For some occasions (eg. a pre-prepared (or "stacked") trick of a routine) you are able to produce the bridged card prior to the performance in which you are going to use it. In which case, if the pre-prepared trick you are going to use it for allows it, once you have created the bridged card cut it into the middle of the pack before placing the pack in its carton.

You should note that only a very slight bridge is required to produce the desired outcome and that during performance (particularly after riffle shuffles) it may be necessary to "refresh" the bridge.

HANDLING A BRIDGED CARD

To cut the bridged card from within the pack hold the pack loosely, the outer end towards the spectators, with the face of the cards facing outwards and the backs inwards.

The thumb is very loosely on the top side of the pack and the fingers are gently supporting the bottom side from beneath. The other hand (again very gently) rests on the pack, the thumb at the inside end and the fingers at the outer end. The pressure of the thumb on the top side of the pack is relaxed, and the pack is allowed to open at the natural break. The bottom section of the pack will fall into the palm of the hand. You lift away this bottom packet of the pack and place it face-down on top of the pack. This should put the bridged card to the bottom of the re-constituted pack. It is prudent, however, to check that this has been achieved and this can be done by glimpsing the card at the bottom of the pack. To do this, after you have completed the cut, turn the face-down pack so that the back of the cards are towards the spectators with the sides of the cards at top and bottom. Hold the pack with both hands, the back of the hands towards the spectators and with the thumbs on the face of the pack and the fingers on the back of the pack. Tap the bottom side of the pack on the table to square up the cards and, in doing so, glimpse the identity of the bottom card. Once you have done so turn the pack face-down and place it on the table. If you do not glimpse the required card have the pack cut again or cut the pack yourself and repeat the whole procedure.

To allow the pack to be cut and to then restore it to its original order begin with the bridged card at the bottom of the face-down pack and allow the pack to be cut and completed. Then cut the bridged card to the bottom of the pack as described in the previous paragraph. To control a selected card which has been returned to either the top or the bottom of the pack after the pack has been cut and completed begin with the bridged card at the bottom of the pack and allow a spectator to replace his or her selected card on the top or at the bottom of the pack. Then allow the spectator to cut and complete the pack as many times as he or she wishes. If you then cut the bridged card to the bottom of the pack the selected card will be the top card of the pack.

To control a selected card returned to the "the middle of the pack" after the pack has been cut and completed begin with the bridged card at the bottom of the pack. Cut off the top half of the face-down pack and place it face-down on the table in front of the spectator. He or she places the selected card on top of this packet and you place what was the bottom half of the pack on top of the selected card. The spectator may now cut and complete, at will. Finally, you cut the bridged card to the bottom of the pack, which places the selected card at the top of the pack. Alternatively, with the pack in hand, cut off the top half of the pack with the other hand and hold this packet face-down towards the spectator for him or her to place the selected card on top of it. Then place what was the bottom of the pack face-down on top of the spectator's card. You then proceed as described above, allowing the spectator to cut and complete before you finally cut the bridged card to the bottom of the pack.

To disguise the use of a bridged card or to retain a card or block of cards at the top of the pack, having cut the bridged card to the bottom of the pack begin the procedure again. This time, in relaxing the pressure of the thumb on the top side of the pack, allow approximately the bottom $^1/_3$ of the pack to fall away into the palm. Now using the index finger of the other hand you open the top $^2/_3$ of the pack as if opening a book and insert what was the bottom $^1/_3$ of the pack into the gap thus formed and then close the pack. The bridged card is now approximately $^2/_3$ of the way down the pack. Repeat this procedure allowing the cards **below** the bridged card to fall into the palm of your hand. As you did before open up a gap in the other cards and place the cards from your palm in it. When the pack is closed the bridged card will be at the bottom of the pack.

THE FALSE SHUFFLE

The simplest false shuffle is what is normally described as the "optical shuffle". If it is performed confidently and smoothly, without looking at the hands or attracting the attention of the spectators to the hands, it is a very deceptive false shuffle. To perform it begin with the pack in position for an overhand shuffle as described earlier in this chapter. Cut away about the bottom $^2/_3$ of the pack and, as in the genuine overhand shuffle, move this packet over the top of the other packet. Do so until it completely covers the other packet without relaxing your grip of it. As the cut-away packet moves over the packet that was the top of the pack place the thumb of the hand holding this packet on top of the cut-off packet, then take the bottom $^2/_3$ you cut-off upwards, as you do so allowing the thumb to slip along the top card of the upward moving packet **but do not release any cards from the packet**. Once the packet has cleared what was the bottom $^1/_3$ of the pack move it down behind that packet and allow a small block of cards to fall onto the bottom of that packet. Continue the procedure until all the cards from what was the bottom part of the pack have been placed behind what was the top $^1/_3$ of the pack. The illusion of a true shuffle can be heightened by, when the $^2/_3$ packet is moved behind the $^1/_3$ packet, the cards of the $^1/_3$ packet are allowed to tilt towards the thumb of the hand holding them.

Another straight-forward and effective false shuffle again begins with the cards in the position for an overhand shuffle. Take about the bottom ¾ of the pack and lift it above the other cards as if beginning a standard overhand shuffle. At the same time the thumb of the lower hand pulls the top ¼ of the pack down onto the fingers of that hand and moves this packet under what was the bottom ¾ of the pack. A break or gap is held between what was the upper ¼ of the pack and what was the bottom ¾ of the pack using the thumb and fingers of the hand holding the pack. Continue pulling of small blocks of cards from the top of what was the bottom ¾ of the pack, placing these blocks beneath what was the top ¼ of the pack, maintaining the gap or break. When all the cards have been transferred the pack will be back in its original order. The secret of success with this false shuffle (which is, in fact, a series of cuts off the top of the pack being transferred to the bottom of the pack in order) is to keep the gap or break as small as possible and to hide it with what was the bottom ¾ of the pack by tilting the pack towards the spectators. The illusion created is of the cards being shuffled into the bottom part of the pack.

The False Cut

If you are using a bridged card the illusion of a fair cut is easily achieved (beginning with the bridged card at the bottom of the pack) by casually cutting and completing the pack two or more times before cutting the bridged card to the bottom of the pack. If, however, you are not using a bridged card or if the bridged card is and must remain within the pack then the illusion must be achieved by other means. One straight-forward (but still deceptive) procedure is to begin with the pack face-down with the outer side towards the spectators. The pack is held with both hands, the thumbs at the inner side and the fingers at the outer side. Tilt the pack, raising the inner side with the thumbs, and then with the right hand pull the bottom $^{1}/_{3}$ of the pack to the right and place it face down on the top of the pack, out-jogged on the outer end of the pack by about half an inch. The consequent out-jog at the inner end of the pack is concealed by the back of the left hand. Repeat the movement for the next $^{1}/_{3}$ of the pack from the bottom of the pack – this time placing the cut-off packet directly on top of the out-jogged packet. Now push down with the left little finger on what is the concealed out-jogged bottom $^{1}/_{3}$ of the packet and pull that packet to the right under the pack with the right hand, placing it on the top of the pack. The pack is then in its original order. The procedure when performed quickly and slickly gives the illusion of a genuine cut.

A False Mix of the Pack

The impression can be given that a pack or block of cards is being thoroughly mixed when, in fact, no change is being made in its order. To do this begin with a bridged card at the bottom of the pack or packet and by then performing a Charlier Shuffle as described earlier in this chapter. You may, if you wish, during the shuffle allow a spectator to determine how many cards you take from the top and from the bottom of the pack or packet. Having completed the shuffle you place the pack face-down on the table, cut off the top ¾ of the pack, and place this packet by the side of what was the bottom of the pack (A). Now cut off the top ¾ of the packet you took off A and place these cards by the side of what was this packet (B). Now cut off the top half of the packet you have placed beside B and place it by the side of what was the bottom of this packet (C). The last packet is D. You now have on the table four packets D – C – B – A. Place A on D and B on AD and then invite a spectator to determine whether C is placed on top of or beneath BAD. Do as he or she wishes and then perform a second Charlier Shuffle. Both you and the spectators may now cut and complete, at will. Finally, you cut the bridged card to the bottom of the pack and the pack is then back in its original order.

The mix may be made without using a bridged card if the bottom card of the pack at the beginning of the procedure is secretly noted. Then at the end of the procedure the pack is turned face-up and spread to show the mix of the cards. When the pack is cut to place the noted card at what will be the bottom of the face-down pack then the pack will have been restored to its original order (*see the section on "Using A Key Card" later in this chapter.*)

THE DOUBLE LIFT

The generally accepted method of performing a double lift is to begin with the outer end of the pack or packet facing the spectators. The cards are held across the palm of the hand with the thumb along the outer side, extending just a little beyond the corner. The four fingers curl around the inner side of the cards. The other hand (palm down) moves over the cards, the fingers at the outer end, the thumb at the inner end. This allows the thumb of this hand to lift the top two cards of the pack or packet to form a small break at the inner end, and this break is immediately taken up by the little finger of the lower hand. At this stage, if it is so wished, the upper hand may be removed and the pack or packet displayed without revealing the break, particularly if when the pack or packet is displayed the outer end is slightly raised.

The lift is made by the thumb of the hand holding the cards sliding from its position at the outer corner to a position on top of the pack or packet, pressing down the middle of the top card. As this movement is being made the other hand (palm down) moves over the cards taking up the same position as described in the previous paragraph. In a combined movement the thumb of the lower hand begins to push the top two cards towards the inner side of the pack or packet while the fingers and thumb of the upper hand assist the movement exerting sufficient pressure to maintain the two cards in alignment. The illusion created is that only one card (the top card) is being moved. In fact, the top two cards are being moved as one. The thumb of the lower hand continues to exert a downward pressure on the middle of the cards.

When the two cards (aligned as one) have been moved approximately half-way across the pack or packet the upper hand is turned palm-up. The fingers of the upper hand now move to beneath the top two cards (still aligned as one) and the thumb of this hand moves to the top of the two cards. The top two cards are then being held in alignment and on the pack by the fingers and thumb of the upper hand, allowing the thumb of the lower hand to slide off the cards onto the top of the other cards of the pack or packet. The cards continue to be moved across the pack or packet and sufficient pressure is exerted on them to produce a convex curve to the face of the cards. As the cards reach the end of the movement across the pack or packet they will abut against the fingers of the lower hand, which are used as a fulcrum to allow the two cards (still aligned as one) to be flipped over and dropped as one onto the cards being held in the lower hand. This will display the face of the second card.

The whole process is now repeated to place the cards back face-down on the pack or packet.

The position that has now been achieved is that the spectator believes that the top face-down card of the pack or packet is what is in fact the second card from the top of the pack or packet, and the performer may take whatever advantage he or she wishes from this misconception.

The essence of the illusion is to ensure that the two cards are maintained in perfect alignment throughout the whole procedure.

A second method of performing the double lift, although less natural, ensures that any mis-alignment on the initial lift is hidden from the spectator. Using this method you begin with the cards in exactly the same position as in the method already described. However, in this second method, once the thumb of the upper hand has secured the break at the inner end of the pack or packet, the inner ends of the top two cards (aligned as one) are lifted by the thumb about ½" off the pack. At the same time the fingers of this hand move onto the top of the two cards, firmly pressing the outer ends of the cards down on the top of the pack, and then pulling the cards along the length of the pack. When the cards have been pulled approximately half-way along the top of the pack they are turned over as one still maintaining their movement along the pack until what was the outer end of the two cards is a little beyond the inner end of the pack. Throughout this movement the fingers of the lower hand and the thumb of the lower hand maintain the alignment of the two cards at the sides and the fingers of the upper hand maintain the alignment of the cards at their outer end by the pressure they are exerting on the cards. The thumb of the upper hand maintains the alignment of the inner end of the cards. The thumb of the upper hand now slides along the top of the cards to pick up the slight extension of the two cards at the inner end of the pack while the fingers of this hand maintain the alignment of the outer end. You should note that, throughout, the position of the fingers and thumb of the upper hand hide any possible mis-alignment of the ends from the spectators, and the thumb and fingers of the lower hand hide any mis-alignment at the sides. You are now in a position to turn the two cards face-down on the pack using the same procedure as described above for the initial turn. However, if so wished, they may be turned face-down using the turn-over described in the first version of the lift.

If the trick being performed requires it, it is possible to lift three, or even four cards, as one. However, the more cards that are lifted the more their alignment (and thickness) becomes problematical and the more likely it is that the spectator will detect the subterfuge. Nevertheless, the double lift (if not over-used) is a most powerful tool for creating some very strong effects.

USING A KEY CARD

A key card is used to allow the performer to locate and, if necessary, to manipulate the position of an unknown card placed in the pack by a spectator. If it is used to locate and identify the unknown card the performer ensures that when the unknown card is placed in the pack the key card (of which the performer knows the identity) is placed next to it or in a known proximity to it. The manipulations required to allow this to be done are the same as are described for handling a bridged card when a selected card is placed in "the middle of the pack" and when the key card is the original bottom card of the face-down pack. What is then required to identify the unknown card is for the performer to spread the cards face-up to show the mix of the cards and to identify the unknown card by its position in relation to the key card. The manipulation to move the now identified card to a position advantageous for the performer is again achieved as with a bridged card, ie. the pack is cut so that the key card will be the bottom card of the pack when the pack is turned face-down. This will place the selected card as the top card of the face-down pack.

The essential skill required by the performer is the ability to spread and cut the pack when it is face-up without arousing any suspicion in the spectator. If the cards are spread from right to left with the thumb of the right hand, pushing each card under the preceding card, then the selected card will be immediately above the key card and must be quickly pulled out of view under the preceding cards. If the cards are spread from right to left as described paragraph 9e for the trick "*Card Sharper's Aces*", sliding the cards with the fingers of the left hand from the bottom of the pack with each card moving above the preceding card, then the key card will be located first and the selected card can be hidden by suppressing it in the spread. In this case, of course, the performer will not be able to identify the selected card. He or she will, however, be able to position it as the top card of the face-down pack.

SOURCES AND BACKGROUND

THIS CHAPTER DESCRIBES THE genesis of each of the tricks that can be used to make up a "*Magic Aces*" routine. It discusses the principles and the mechanics underpinning the tricks and, where appropriate, acknowledges the sources which provided the initial inspiration for the effect or suggested the means by which particular effects could be achieved.

Finding The Aces

This trick is composed of a series of forces based on the fact that if you take a block of cards and cut off from it 10 to 19 cards, count out those cards reversing their order, and then go to the card in the counted-out cards corresponding to the number derived by adding the two digits of the counted-out number together, then the card arrived at will be the card that was the 10th from the top in the original block of cards.

A few calculations illustrate the principle involved:

$(10 = 1 + 0 = 1)$ and $(10 - 1 = 9)$
$(15 = 1 + 5 = 6)$ and $(15 - 6 = 9)$
$(18 = 1 + 8 = 9)$ and $(18 - 9 = 9)$

In other words the number of cards remaining in the block of cards after the second count will always be nine, and these cards will be the original top nine cards of the block.

The forcing of the first Ace in the trick is a straightforward application of this principle.

The forcing of the second Ace is an application of the same principle with the performer controlling the size of the block of cards removed.

The principle can be extended to allow for blocks of cards larger than 19 to be used. However, in these cases the position of the card to be forced has to be appropriately adjusted, the reason being that the underlying principle is that for any two digit number if the two digits are added together and the single digit figure arrived at is subtracted from the original number then the final number arrived at will always be a multiple of 9.

Again a few calculations illustrate this:

$(23 = 2 + 3 = 5)$ $(23 - 5 = 18)$ $(9 \times 2 = 18)$
$(35 = 3 + 5 = 8)$ $(35 - 8 = 27)$ $(9 \times 3 = 27)$
$(47 = 4 + 7 = 11)$ $(47 - 11 = 36)$ $(9 \times 4 = 36)$

Again the multiple of 9 will always be the number of cards remaining in the block after the second count. Thus in a block of 20-29 cards the card to be forced requires to be at the 19th position from the top in the original block, in a block of 30-39 cards at the 28th position, and in a 40-49 block at the 37th position.

The forcing of the third Ace in the trick follows from the fact that at the beginning of the second force there are 19 cards above the third Ace. 18 of these cards are returned to the top of the pack and these cards remain in hand on the force:

$(25 = 2 + 5 = 7)$ and $(25 - 7 = 18)$
$(27 = 2 + 7 = 9)$ and $(27 - 9 = 18)$
$(29 = 2 + 9 = 11)$ and $(29 - 11 = 18)$

It would be possible to force the fourth Ace using the same principle but three forces using the same procedure are enough and, in any case, the arrangement for the fourth Ace to be produced from the bottom of the pack provides just as strong, perhaps even stronger, a finish.

A full description of the straight-forward Four Card Force can be found at page 188 of the book "*Expert Card Techniques*" (Dover Publications Inc., New York, 1974) by Jean Hugard and Frederick Braué, and readers who wish to study further the uses to which mathematical principles can be put in card magic are recommended to see the books "*Card Concepts*" (Lewis Davenport, London, 2004) by Arthur F. MacTier and Martin Gardner's "*Mathematics, Magic, and Mystery*" (Dover Publications Inc., New York, 1956). In this latter book the reader will be interested to note at page 20 a description of a trick in which the principle used for my trick "*Finding The Aces*" is applied in a different way. It is a four Ace trick, ascribed by Martin Gardener to Billy O'Connor, where, before the performance begins, the Aces are secretly placed at the 9th, 10th, 11th, and 12th positions from the top of the pack. The performer then invites a spectator to choose any number between 10 and 20 and, once this number has been chosen, he or she deals out that number of cards face-down onto the table from the top of the face-down pack. The two digits of the chosen number are then added together to give a single digit number and the number of cards corresponding to this number are dealt off the top of the pile on the table. These cards are then placed on top of the pack. When the top card of *the pile* is turned over the first Ace is revealed. It is removed from the pile and placed on the table. The performer then places what were the remaining cards of the dealt-out pile on top of the pack and continues the trick, going through the same procedure to reveal the second, then the third, and then the fourth Ace. The handling and the secret positioning of the Aces, of course, ensure that when the cards corresponding to the calculated number are returned to the pack there will always be nine cards on the table, and the top card of this pile will be an Ace.

You Must Be Joking

This trick combines a number of ways of handling the cards to produce a surprising and amusing effect. The impression created is that the cards are being thoroughly mixed, particularly when the cards are riffle shuffled together. In fact, neither the cutting of the cards nor the shuffles in any way alters the position of the Aces or the Jokers in relation to each other.

The riffle shuffle is a most useful handling device in card manipulation in that when the two parts of the pack are inter-weaved the order of the cards in the two parts is maintained. In addition, the shuffle allows the performer to retain cards at the top and/or at the bottom of the pack as he or she wishes. Both these characteristics of the shuffle are fully utilised in the performance of the trick to control the location of the Aces and the Jokers within the pack.

For some interesting uses to which the riffle shuffle can be put the reader may care to see Karl Fulves' book "*More Self-Working Card Tricks*" (Dover Publications Inc., New York, 1984, pages 45-56).

Card Sharper's Aces

This is a mini-routine in its own right combining a number of tricks drawing their inspiration from several sources.

The first part of the trick involving the initial dealing out of the Aces is based on the classic "*Three Jack Deal*". This is described in three versions by Karl Fulves in his book "*Self-Working Close-Up Card Magic*" (Dover Publications Inc., New York, 1995) at pages 75-79: "*Jack, Jack, Jack*", "*Three Jacks Improved*", and "*Unstacked Jacks*".

There are some intrinsic weaknesses in the basic trick as described in "*Jack, Jack, Jack*". The first is that the trick requires a pre-arrangement of five cards, ie., Jack, Jack, Jack, any card, Jack, at the top of the pack; the second is that it is necessary to use the subterfuge of "scooping up" the dealer's undisplayed cards using the last undisplayed card dealt to ensure that when those cards are placed back on top of the pack with the spectator's displayed Jacks placed face-down on them the original pre-arrangement is re-created; and the third is that when the performer goes to the second deal the colour combination of the revealed Jacks may differ from deal to deal, e.g. if the first deal produced Red-Red-Black the second deal will produced Black-Black-Red, which is unlikely not to give the spectator a strong inkling as to how the effect is being achieved. To an extent, the "*Three Jacks Improved*" version of the trick, the development of which Fulves ascribes to Walter Gibson, obviates this weakness by ensuring that the only change between the first and second deal is the identity of the Black Jack, but this only at the expense of a more complicated pre-arrangement of the top cards of the pack, ie. Red Jack, Black Jack, Red Jack, any card, Black Jack and an even more complicated subterfuge for picking up the cards to arrange them for the second deal in that in addition to the handling used in the "*Jack, Jack, Jack*" version to place the Jack of the three undisplayed dealer's cards as the middle card of the three, the same handling is used to place the Black Jack of the spectator's three displayed Jacks in the middle of those cards. Jack Potter's version of the trick, to which Fulves gives the title "*Unstacked Jacks*" requires no pre-arrangement of the pack other than placing one Black Jack as the third card in the pack while openly displaying the other three Jacks. Six cards are then inter-leaved by placing the first face-down card from the top of the pack face-down on the table, by then placing the revealed Black Jack face-down on top of it, and by then carrying on this procedure for the two Red Jacks. If these six cards are then placed on top of the pack and the top three cards are dealt out face-up onto the table, they will be two Red Jacks and one Black Jack. Furthermore, if these Jacks (with the Black Jack as the middle card of the three) are replaced face-down on top of the pack then the top cards are set for the "*Jack, Jack, Jack*" version of the trick. The weakness remaining, of course, is that the identity of the Black Jack will still alter from deal to deal. Accepting this weakness, it is on Jack Potter's version of the trick that I have based my own.

There is, however, yet another weakness in all the versions of the trick as described by Fulves which is that at no time during the performance of the trick are all six cards displayed (or rather, apparently displayed) to the spectator. My own version, using the double lift to conceal the second Black Ace, is a means of over-coming this weakness. Furthermore, in my version of the trick no subterfuge is required to re-set the pre-arrangement for the second deal.

The second part of the trick, the dealing out of the Poker hands, is set up by demonstration of how the hands will be dealt. This places the Aces in a configuration to allow the spectator a free choice of cards in the actual deal. On the assumption that it might be of interest and use to the reader a method that can be used to determine the required pre-arrangement is set out below:

ORDER	1	2	3	4	5	6	7	8	9	10
CARD	X	A	X	A	A	X	X	X	X	A

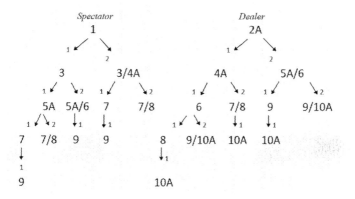

Telepathic Aces

This trick depends for its success on the method used to identify the cards around which the Aces are placed in the Miniature pack or in the first full-sized pack if the Miniature pack is not used.

The method is usually referred to as "*the pump action*", "*the push-pull effect*", or "*the piston effect*" and it is normally used by the performer to produce a selected card rising from within the pack. Here, however, the effect is reversed and concealed to allow the performer to identify a card.

The use of the piston effect to produce a rising card is attributed in most books on card magic to Jack McMillen.

Just Think of An Ace

Spelling out a selected card always creates a strong impression on spectators, spelling out a card that has only been thought of by a spectator even more so. The trick "*Just Think of An Ace*", which does this, is based on the fortunate fact that the number of letters in the spelling out of the Aces can be manipulated to produce a sequence: "Ace of Clubs" (10), "Ace of Hearts" (11), "Ace of Diamonds" (13). Thus any one of them can be spelled out by taking the card placed at the appropriate position of the final "s" of the spelling. "Ace of Spades" (11) can be accommodated into the sequence by placing it between "Ace of Hearts" (11) and "Ace of Diamonds" (13) and by taking the card left on the top of the pack when "Ace of Spades" is spelled out, ie. the 12th card. The essence of the trick therefore becomes the handling required to place the Aces in their appropriate positions.

A version of this trick under the title "*Think of An Ace*" can be found in my own book, "*Old Wine In A New Bottle*" (Trafford, Bloomington, 2010).

All Together Now

This trick is based on a principle developed by Simon Aronson and described in his book "*Bound To Please*" (Aronson, Chicago, 1994). It is also discussed by Arthur F. MacTier in his "*Card Concepts*" (Davenport, London, 2000). The principle is that if a pack of cards is divided into two packets and if a number of cards from each packet are turned over and shuffled into the other packet and this process is repeated as many times as wished, then, if, finally, one of the packets is turned over and shuffled into the other packet, the pack will contain the original two packets, one face-up and the other face-down.

In the trick "*All Together Again*" the Aces constitute a face-down packet and the rest of the cards a face-up packet. The fact that the packet contains cards with differently coloured backs significantly heightens the impression that the pack is being thoroughly mixed.

A possible weakness in the performance of the trick is that if the shuffles are not controlled it is possible that the spectator in shuffling his or her packet will note and be suspicious of the face-up Aces in the packet. This weakness is over-come by the handling suggested for the trick ensuring that for all the shuffles the face-up Aces will always be in the performer's packet and that the Aces in the spectator's packet will always be face-down.

Magic Clocks

Versions of this effect can be found in many books on card magic. Karl Fulves describes one version, "*Crazy Clocks*" at pages 14-16 in his book "*More Self-Working Card Magic*" (Dover, New York, 1984). It depends for its working on the performer knowing the identity of the 13th card down from the top of the pack. Knowing this card the performer is in a position to predict that it will be this card that will eventually be chosen by the spectator. To produce this outcome the performer begins by inviting the spectator to think of any hour on a clock face. The spectator then secretly removes from the top of the pack the number of cards corresponding to the hour he or she has selected and hides them away. The performer then deals out into a face-down pile on the table the top 12 cards of the pack and then takes these cards and deals them out face-up to form the face of the clock. The spectator is then invited to declare his or her chosen hour and to note the card at that hour on the clock face. It will be the card predicted by the performer.

Fulves strengthens the presentation of the trick by suggesting that the performer should write his or her prediction on a slip of paper which is handed to the spectator at the beginning of the performance, and by also writing the selected hour on a second slip of paper once he or she has seen the position of the known card in the lay-out of the clock face. Additionally, Fulves notes that if the performer identifies not only the 13th card in the pack but also the 25th then he or she may place aside all the cards used in the first part of the trick to form the face of the clock, replace the spectator's cards on top of the pack, and repeat the trick using as the prediction the identity of this 25th card.

I had a number of reservations about the mechanics of the trick as described by Fulves. The first was the necessity for the performer to identify the 13th card in the pack, the second was the counting off of the cards by the spectator, the third was that in forming the clock face the cards were placed face-up, and the fourth was that to prepare for the forming of the clock face the order of the cards had to be reversed by dealing them out and then dealing them into a clock face.

In my version of the trick the performer is required to know the top card of the pack. This opens up the possibility of easily controlling the return of any selected card to that position or easily positioning any required card at that position. The problem then is how to use this top card in the clock effect. The solution I decided upon was to deal out a 12-card packet of cards from which the spectator could remove an unknown number of cards, leaving the original top card of the pack at the bottom of the cards not taken by the spectator. If these cards were then used as the top cards of a new 12-card packet then the position of the original top card of the pack in the clock face would be the number of cards cut off by the spectator, provided that the cards were dealt out in reverse order (thus the requirement to construct the clock face in an anti-clockwise direction beginning at 11 o'clock). Finally, the cards forming the clock face could be dealt out face-down. All that was then required was to disguise the mechanism of the trick by a sequence of false cuts and false mixes.

I also thought that the trick could be strengthened by using two clock faces simultaneously and thus involving two spectators.

The positioning of the Aces does involve a somewhat complicated handling technique but the resulting effect more than justifies this.

Spell Them Out

It has already been noted that the Aces can be arranged in such a way that, once they are appropriately positioned within the pack, they may be spelled out (*see the section on "Just Think of An Ace" earlier in this chapter.*) This trick, "*Spell Them Out*", extends this effect to two packs and directly involves three spectators.

The trick depends for its success on the handling of the cards to position the Aces.

It might be thought that the suggested handling is over-complicated. However, if it is studied carefully and practised diligently, it will be found to be not as complicated or forbidding as it appears at first sight. In any case, my own view is that the effect achieved more than justifies the procedure required to produce it.

More Aces

The first part of this trick, ie. the position of the Aces as the top cards of each of the packets, is a variation of a trick described by Jean Hugard in his book "*The Royal Road To Card Magic*" (Dover, New York, 1999) under the title "*A Poker Player's Picnic*". In Hugard's version the spectator is directed to take each pile of cards in turn and to transfer three cards from the top of the pile to the bottom of the pile and then to take the next three cards from the top of the pile and place one on top of each of the other piles. Provided the final pile started with the four Aces as its top cards it follows that all the piles will finish with an Ace as the top card.

My suggested finish for the trick is a series of top card forces.

The first is what is usually referred to as "*The X Force*" or "*The Cross Card Force*". It depends for its success on there being a reasonable interval of time (filled with distraction) between the cut being made and the forced card being revealed. The second force is merely a variation of the same force using a little more finesse.

The third force is a variation on what is known as the "*Cut Deeper Force*" developed by Ed Balducci. In its original form it places the card to be forced from the top of the pack to a position as the first face-down card in the pack. This is achieved by inviting the spectator to take the face-down pack, to cut off about the top ¼ of the pack, to turn those cards over and to place them on top of the rest of the pack. He or she is then invited to cut off about the top ½ of the pack, to turn those cards over, and to place them on top of the pack. In my variation the card to be forced will, at the end of the procedure, still be the top face-down card of the packet.

The fourth force, although very simple in execution, is very deceptive in terms of outcome, particularly as there is a delay between the forcing of the card and its revelation.

Everybody's Ace

A classic trick in the armoury of the performer of card magic is "*Everybody's Card*". It requires the forcing of the same card onto as many spectators as the performer wishes to involve and then arranging for them all to realise simultaneously that they have all chosen the same card. It depends for its success on a series of forces – preferably a series in which each force is different from all those which precede it.

In my book "*Old Wine In A New Bottle*" (Trafford, Bloomington, 2010) I suggest that a bridged card should be used as the card to be forced. This simplifies the performance, but adapting the trick to force the same Ace onto each spectator requires a different technique and for "*Everybody's Ace*" I have described four forces that can be used. These, when combined with the initial locating of the Ace, produce the required outcome.

The first force requires the performer to place an Ace face-down at the top of the face-down pack. In some circumstances, particularly where the performer assesses that the spectators are not paying a great deal of attention to the handling of the pack, this can be done with very little subterfuge being required. However, there are a number of techniques that can be used to disguise the move and one of these is set out in detail at paragraph 2 of the description of the trick "*Magic Clocks*" in the chapter "*Adaptations and Alternatives*".

The second force is a variation of the "*Cut Deeper Force*" used in the previous trick "*More Aces*". It places the card to be forced from the top of the pack as the first face-down card in the pack. The third force is yet a further variation of the same force.

The fourth and final force appears to be yet another variation of that used in the trick "*Finding The Aces*". In this case, however, the force is using a totally different mechanism to lead to the required card. It is, in fact, merely a complicated (and, therefore, a deceiving) way of placing on top of the card to be forced the same number of cards cut off by the spectator.

The successful forcing of a card has always been an essential skill in performing tricks with cards and from the very beginnings of card magic to the present day performers have been devising methods to achieve it.

Readers might be interested to know that in one of his books Theodore Annemann describes over two hundred techniques for forcing not only cards but also numbers, colours, names, coins, and a variety of other objects: "*202 Methods of Forcing*" (Davenport, London, 1994). The techniques range from the so-called "*Classic Force*", the success of which depends purely upon the skill of the performer to coincide the position of the required card in a spread pack with the grasping fingers of the spectator's advancing hand, to methods that are mechanical and self-working – a number of which are, to say the least, bizarre. They do, however, all work!